MW01171655

7 Ways To Change Your Life
by (B)eing (E)xcellent (N)ow

7 Ways To Change Your Life by (B)eing (E)xcellent (N)ow

Benjamin H.S. Scott Jr.

THE BRAG MEDIA COMPANY
LAGOS. NEWYORK. LONDON.

7 WAYS TO CHANGE YOUR LIFE
BY (B)EING (E)XCELLENT (N)OW.

Copyright © 2020
by **Benjamin H.S. Scott Jr.**

━━━━━━━━━━━

All rights reserved. No part of
this publication may be reproduced,
distributed, or transmitted in any
form or by any means, including
photocopying, recording, or other
electronic or mechanical methods,
without the prior written
permission of the author, except
in the case of brief quotations
embodied in critical reviews and
certain other noncommercial uses
permitted by copyright law.

Published by The BRAG Media Company

━━━━━━━━━━━

This book may be ordered from book-sellers or, contact...
www.BenScottLLC.com

Printed in the United States
ISBN: 979-8-619987720

Contents

Introduction

We all want to change something in our lives, but we sometimes get stuck on the how. I want to give you 7 ways to jump-start your new way of thinking. One of the best ways to start your brand-new way of thinking centers around (B.E.N) Be Excellent Now. This statement is smooth, and the concept is simple, but that does not mean it is easy to do. But it can be done.

We are all self-made. For the most part, we are where we are in life as a result of our actions, and those actions are a result of our habits, and those habits were formed from our Mindsets.

I realized that I wanted to be, and do something else, as a result of my time in Iraq. I had been in the military for right at 20 years, and I realized I was stuck.

I loved my job, but I was beginning to understand that I was capable of more; much more than I was producing. I had once again in my life, settled for being good enough.

I witnessed the aftermath of our Tomahawk Cruise missiles, destroying everything in sight. And, we fired more than 40 of these powerfully destructive tools of war. Those weapons did their assigned missions extremely well. Coming in behind a US Infantry Division's devastation of its foe was a sight I will never forget.

I was in a location that had run out of water. It was more than 100 degrees outside, with nearly 90% humidity. We had no fixed housing, or bathrooms, and toilet paper at times were nonexistent. The only things I looked forward to were letters and mail from my family and friends. Those care boxes filled the needs where our supply system couldn't meet. My family was my motivation, and the main reason I succeeded in my mission there.

From my time in that combat zone, I realized that I could be in heaven, while in hell, or in hell, while in heaven; either of these feelings is a choice – it is a Mindset. For most of us, happiness is just that, a choice!

While in Iraq, I saw some of the children who had no running water or shoes, and they were happy. They played games with made-up balls, and they lived. I say again, happiness is a choice, no matter the circumstance that you are in. Once you choose to be happy, your life will absolutely change.

When I returned from Iraq, I was angry and destructive. I literally broke most things around me. That was when I was introduced to the power of positive thinking. I started learning that what I thought; I became. I no longer wanted to be angry, so I channeled that rage into action. I became more B.E.N through my pain, and I have never looked back. These 7 steps that I will introduce and teach can help you become more of your excellent self. If applied, they will change you, as well as those around you.

I made myself someone less than I was capable of

being, "good enough," for many years. I did this for several reasons. One was the lack of belief in myself.

At times, I didn't think I was worthy, so I accepted the negative things people said about me as fact. The second I realized that their truth was not my own, my world changed. Read this carefully. If you don't like where you are in your life, change your Mindset! Make today, make right now, the start of your new tomorrow that you want.

I believe that 80% of our "unhappy times" is because we allow someone else's ideas about who we are to define us. I want you to stop that thinking today! Anything that is imaginable for one, is possible for you. Do your homework and find the power within yourself. I say again, we are all self-made! You define YOU.

We blame others for our faults when we can't confront ownership of where we are. One of my goals for this book is to help you wake up and realize – you made you, and you are making the future you right now. Who do you want your future self to be? Who is the best version of your future self? These 7 steps will help you to get to that realization. The realization that your best can always be better, and if you know you aren't where you are supposed to be, change those aspects you need to change and Be Excellent Now!

1.

What Is Your Legacy?

We have all the time in the world, but only the time in this world.

"Carpe Diem" means seize the day. I also translate this thought process to mean doing what we have to do in order to be our best selves. We are all self-made, and we are making ourselves and revising our future with each action we undertake.

It is important to put pressure on ourselves; we have to get things done quickly without sacrificing quality. Things must be accomplished swiftly because there is a time limit on our life span. There is a time stamp on our physicality and a time limit on our beauty as well as neuroplasticity. Even if we don't acknowledge it, we know it. It's important—no, imperative – to capitalize on our gifts as soon as possible. Our most valuable asset is also our most wasted asset – TIME.

Acknowledging that we have a time limit can help us capitalize on the time we have. Ask yourself, how can you speed up your learning process in order to achieve more, in less time? One of the best ways is not to repeat the mistakes of others. Understanding and implementing this will put you well ahead of those peers who are doing discovery learning.

Looking, listening, and feeling at what others have endured will help you navigate your journey quicker and with more effectiveness. That is where mentorship and coaching need to be leveraged.

Finding someone with like-minded values who is already ahead of you on the "track", will help you make your dreams a reality in a shorter time than most, and with fewer headaches along the way. Mentorship is different than coaching.

A coach can give you distinct techniques, ideas, and thought processes that can be used to get ahead. They also hold you accountable for the utilization of those techniques, ideas and/or thought processes.

A mentor can nourish those ideas, as well as teach and guide you from their own experiences.

The greats have both mentors and coaches. The coach and the mentor don't have to be the same person, but if you choose, they can be one and the same.

Usually, our first mentor and coach is a family member. For me, my maternal grandmother was my special coach and mentor. She was my confidant; someone I could rely on, and she always provided the best tasting food with that exceptional grandmamma love.

One of the most vivid memories I have of her is "bacon". Yup, bacon—not the smell of cooking bacon, but how many pieces we got.

My grandmother always cooked breakfast on the weekend, and I always look forward to those weekends!!! She worked very long and hard hours, and her devotion to her religious beliefs was exceptional.

She served as a maid during my childhood among other odd jobs to add income to the family of five. We all lived in a one-bathroom two-room house—later a front room was added on to the house.

Breakfast usually consisted of grits, eggs, and bacon. This was, and still is, my favorite breakfast meal. It consisted of 1-2 eggs a plate full of grits and 3 pieces of bacon.

Later in life, I got my own place and made my own breakfast. You know what my favorite meal was/is… grits, eggs and bacon. I had my plate full of grits, my two eggs and my three pieces of bacon. However, what I found odd was that my bacon pieces were always so much larger than my grandmamma's.

I just couldn't understand why my bacon was so much bigger than hers. I mean, yes I was able to get a better quality of the bacon and even the thicker cuts. But how come my slices were so much bigger.

Then, I realized it!!!! My grandmamma was cutting the bacon in half for our family so that it could be stretched to feed all five of us.

That is so poignant to me. How far my family has come and yet how much farther we can go. I am a Legacy of The Scotts and the Wares!!!!

Now, I throw away packets of bacon that have been in the refrigerator for too long and think nothing of it. I don't even think about how much a packet of bacon costs.

Again, she was cutting a pack in half so that it

could stretch so that everyone could have some. As a little kid, all I knew was, there was always three pieces. That is a powerful illustration of the child-like innocence in us, versus the adult cognition that we learn with age. Yet, when as young adults we ingest what others say we are and hold those opinions as "our" truth.

When I found out that we would be moving away from her, I was distraught. My family was moving from Charleston to Illinois and all I knew was, I didn't want to go because my Grandmamma wouldn't be there. My father was being stationed on a new base, and as a kid, I had no choice in the matter. My first memory of emotional pain was leaving her.

My grandmother's passing really made me aware of the limited, short life span that we have. She was a staple in our family to me. She was a force, and we all looked up to her. She was a constant and motivational force in my life, and the loss of her changed me.

The day I got the notification of her passing, I had mixed feelings about it. She was unable to communicate for many years. She was a beautiful person stuck in a body that she could not fully utilize. She was my refuge, and her loss of speech and impaired motor functions angered and saddened me.

One of my biggest regrets, to this day, is not communicating with her as often as I could. I was so self-absorbed and even weak. I can recall the deep emotions of pain and regret I felt when I got the message she had passed while I was stationed in Germany. I remember the empty feeling I felt in the pit of my stomach, and in my heart at my loss. I was completely floored, by her passing. I started crying, throwing and breaking things.

I clearly remember breaking a drinking glass the in wake of my loss. In the aftermath of my rage, it was time to clean things up. Because I did not have a mop or broom, I recall cleaning up all the glass and liquid on the floor with a towel. Later, I washed and dried the towel during the laundry day. That night was not a peaceful rest.

A few weeks later, after getting out of the shower, I used that same towel, the one I had cleaned the floor and re-washed, to dry myself. I felt a little scratch on my skin but continued – then a full-fledged cut. Now, you may recall, I washed and dried this towel already. So, I thought that since I had washed the towel, there wouldn't be any glass pieces would be left behind to worry about—wrong.

When we make messes in our lives and try to clean them up, we have to use the right tools and do a thorough cleaning. When we don't, we leave a residue, or we don't get the full intended result. When we don't thoroughly investigate, find, and clean up the messes that we've made, we may leave a disaster in our wake.

After an event happens, we can respond or react. My reaction to learning of my grandmamma's passing was to tear thing up – to be destructive. I had a choice, and I made a bad one. After all the dust had settled, I tried to clean up that choice and found that even though I had cleaned; I had residual pieces of glass left. I did not do a thorough job.

Pieces of glass were left because I used the wrong tools and didn't clean my mess up thoroughly. Even if I didn't use the right tool (towel vs broom and mop), maybe I should have thrown that tool away, because it was too badly damaged from being used incorrectly.

In our lives, we make messes; it is nearly inevitable. Understanding those messes defines us, how we deal with them will become our legacy.

Is there a mess in your life that you didn't properly clean up? And when a mess is made, how are you dealing with the cleanup? Is that person, place, or thing still a part of your life? We often have people that we need to stop dealing, hanging, or associating with.

Look at the four or five people that you know for certain are not bringing value to your life, the way in which you need. They are a distraction to you. Moving you from your future success – so why do you keep them near you? They are shaping your legacy.

Another bad habit may be your spending habits, what mess have you made in your life that continues to haunt you with your money? It is affecting your legacy.

Sometimes we think too small and that can be a mess all on its own. When we think minuscule, we get small. Where are you thinking too small? It is affecting your legacy.

We all go through things, but we can also grow through them. When we don't clean up messes in our lives, it closes the door to a new opportunity. Sometimes after we have cleaned up a mess, the item that we used to clean up the mess has served its purpose. What habit is no longer serving its purpose? But we hold on to that thing far longer than we should, maybe in hopes that it can still serve a purpose. But more than likely now it is time to let it go.

Think for a moment about your bad habits. We all know what they are—sometimes we just pretend that we don't know.

Let's grow up and deal with our drama. Challenge: Figure out what you need to clean up in your life? Identify it, write it down, and make a plan to fix it. It is also important to find someone to help hold you accountable for the change you know you need to make. Because it is affecting your legacy.

Our life is finite in this world. However, one definition of life is forever. The soul will live forever, but the body will not.

In this life, in this world, we only have this time!

A core principle that we should recognize is that this life is "our legacy". We must acknowledge that we are leaving a legacy. What is your legacy saying about you?

My goal is to always be the best at whatever I decide to do. I may not reach the goal of being number one, but I will always be in the top ten percent. My son is a part of my legacy, as is my work. I was a Command Sergeant Major, which will forever be a part of my legacy. I am forever and always building my legacy. You, too, are always building your legacy.

My mindset is to impact everyone I interact with. You may forget my name, but you will always remember the emotional impact I had on your life. The impression that I leave when you meet me lasts.

There is also a dark side to our legacy. We all have made mistakes in life. We must acknowledge our mistakes in order to improve our present and our future. We must acknowledge that the mistakes we have made will last. The goal, however, is to do what you can to fix your mistakes.

There are turmoil and dark sides everywhere, and yes that includes, inside of you and me. If others can learn from my errors and mistakes and not make them, I will have made a positive impact and left the world better than I found it.

In building our legacy, we must be cognizant of those around us that can be affected by our truth. Know that we are not islands unto ourselves. Be mindful of revealing your thoughts and the impact that those truths may have on others. Remember, we all leave things in our wake. We must think about the impact that we are leaving behind.

I often ask my coaching clients, "How will you be eulogized?". It is said that once we die, we are loved for one generation, missed for two, and forgotten in the third. Think about how powerful that is for a moment.

I believe the three most important things in life are relationships, health, and wealth. When you are on your deathbed, you are contemplating if the ones that you loved knew you loved them.

Anyone with health issues later in life will spend countless amounts of money to get those issues fixed so they can get their health together.

Wealth provides you with an outlet to get what you want accomplished—it gives you the option.

Never get it twisted – the order is the order!!!

I can't say this enough. We have all the time in the world, but only the time in this world.

We must keep relationships, health, and wealth, uppermost in our minds. This lends to our legacy.

Concentrate on improving those three principles and your legacy will be a success.

Build strong lasting relationships with your God, yourself, and your family, because we all want to be happy.

Protect your health, the health of your family and the health of your co-worker. Health is fragile and yet strong. Protect it.

Increase your wealth, help increase the wealth of your family, and help increase the wealth of your community. Economic freedom equals more choices and opportunities.

Always remember that happiness is a choice so choose wisely.

What is your legacy and what are you doing to improve upon it?

Your Legacy Workbook

1. Define what your legacy will be.

_____
_____
_____
_____
_____
_____
_____

2. What do you want people to say at your funeral?

_____
_____
_____
_____
_____
_____
_____

3. What are you doing to work on your legacy?

_____
_____
_____
_____
_____
_____

_____

4. Who is holding you accountable for it?

_____

_____

_____

_____

_____

_____

_____

5. What time will you set aside to review your legacy?

_____

_____

_____

_____

_____

_____

_____

2.

There is a Time to be Pretty Boy and a Time to be Money Mayweather

In life, you have to understand how to finesse. There is a time and place for everything. We must understand how to assimilate to every situation. That art stems from what I like to call the Pretty Boy vs Money Mayweather method. There is a time to be Floyd "Money Mayweather" and a time to be "Pretty Boy Mayweather". Some saw Pretty Boy Mayweather as loud and obnoxious, and others deemed Money Mayweather as smooth and calculating. There is an appropriate time for each, and that is a part of leadership and winning.

You have to understand what you want in order to win. That requires you being confident in whatever it is that makes you – you. When we don't have confidence, we can't fully become who we are meant to be. Confidence is built. The building of confidence comes from several avenues. One way is by learning from others and practising that which you have learned… Do. Once confidence is built, it will remain; However, lack of confidence may show up in other areas—so, don't be discouraged. Another positive cascading effect of confidence is the trickle-down effect, once gained in one area, it will easily be generated in another.

The art of winning stems from understanding your opponent, and how to get the desired effect you want from them, be it with a situation or yourself. Winning, that word alone gets my pulse jumping. When you win, that feeling of accomplishment, of being a success, of clear domination effervesces over an opponent can be indescribable.

A few questions: How do you a win? How do you define winning? Is it different at home than at work? Is the definition of winning universal?

Here are some possible answers. Leaders set the tone and define winning. You are a Leader. Helping people get little wins under their belt, encourages them to become more confident, which will allow them to become a winner. To that end, recognizing that you are winning right now will add confidence to you and what you are doing.

Winning is individualized. You and I decide what that means to us and if we are winning. Winning requires building confidence, that confidence helps increase the odds of winning. Once you identify and praise those tiny wins, those small victories add up and continually move you closer to your goal.

In situations when I wasn't winning, and I wanted to win, I intentionally built confidence in certain situations by taking deliberate actions.

Growing up, I was told that I was NOT a winner by the outside world. The outside world told me that I was a dark, black, ugly, stupid, Negro that didn't read well 'and would never amount to anything. The outside world meant for these words to germinate and keep me in my place. Most of my family told me the opposite. But as we go into adolescence, which words do we seem to believe and hold on to? The outside world.

Those outside world's words haunted me for a long time and I even watered those negative seeds; later in life they did bear some destructive fruits. Well, until I started to learn and understand confidence and Mind Shift.

At the age of 12, I had a knack for martial arts, which helped me with discipline. Once I leveraged that discipline, confidence arrived, which helped build a bridge to the future that I wanted.

Those hurtful words from the outside world were diminished through the light of discipline and confidence. Confidence helped change my entire existence, and the same can be/is true for you.

I did slip again into the mindset of lack. This was shortly after my first semester in college. After a few years of struggling financially and academically, I decided to join the Army. A great decision and a plan (although I did not fully execute the plan).

Joining the military helped me regain some of the confidence that I lost. Nevertheless, another setback zapped it again. Then a few successes and yet another few disappointments and failures occurred and my confident vision shrank.

We often gain confidence from our craft and the praise we get from doing it well. Doing what we love and getting better at it, brings admiration and praise that pushes us to be our best selves. Do a little research on Michael Jordan. He accomplished many things in his life, but one thing he did not accomplish was making the varsity basketball team for his high school. He turned this challenge into motivation and started practising every day on his own. His discipline led to him becoming a better performer, which led to him being more confident, which led to him being a better performer. The process feeds upon itself. Those that are successful find ways to get around challenges and roadblocks.

The military teaches many great things. It teaches discipline that helps in every aspect of life. The military has Preventive Maintenance Checks and Services (PMCS). It stresses the importance of checking on and taking care of the little things on a routine basis before those little things become a major problem. Note the first word in PMCS—preventive. This also means proactive.

In your personal life, performing a PMCS can prevent potential problems or issues becoming a reality. Performing a PMCS may provide early identification of a major breakdown getting ready to happen in your life. This early detection will give you some time to prepare and mitigate the negative outcomes – the ability to take evasive action. When was the last time you PMCS'd your life? Have you done a check on your relationships, your health, and your wealth? Have you ever asked a relative or close friend "how is our relationship"? That simple check-in can change the core of your relationships.

Relationships are huge when it comes to building confidence and changing your thought process.

Confidence is instilled in us when we are children. When we are young, the little wins that we get praised for usually encourage us to continue that path or even do more.

Take a child's first steps, for example. Even the mere trying to walk is praised over and over. Once that first step is complete, the parents fawn and clap and are overjoyed. The child then learns that that action is rewarded because they are praised for doing it. The small child feels so much love and joy about themselves.

When one is praised, we instinctively feel we are good enough. Once we know what we can do coupled with positive reinforcement, we have the tendency to do more of that which brought us positive attention. Then we become excellent at it through repetition. Excellence is what we long for the most.

The question posed is, how do you build confidence as an adult?

One way is to "do what you say you are going to do". That builds, confidence, self-respect, and self-esteem. Case in point, I needed to get up at 4:20 AM for a new position. I set my alarm for 4:20 and woke up and got up before my alarm. When I got up at that time, I was energized, because I did what I said I was going to do. Once I created that habit for myself, I could get up at that time every morning. My body wakes me up at that time no matter what. The small wins matter. Even a crawl is a step towards your ultimate goal. Even when we stand up and fall down, we are still providing forward momentum. We are sometimes so focused on not achieving the goal that we forget to see and celebrate the things that we have done to reach the current end state. We need to celebrate as we go along and course-correct as necessary.

Confidence is a key and crucial ingredient to success. When I was studying how to attract and date women, yes I did say that. I found confidence was a huge factor. I studied what I wanted to get better at. Anything you want to be improved upon your study. If you want to be better at love or even economics, you should study those topics so that you can be excel at them. I studied how to be more attractive to women because I know that we are visual beings and looks grab our attention at first.

In my research, I found the number-one thing that kept a woman attracted to you was a confident person. Confidence can be judged in many ways: by posture, one's walk, the way one talks, and how one carries themselves and engages with others in conversation and acts. Confidence is paramount. If one is certain, they exude confidence. On the other end of the spectrum, those that are not confident project the exact opposite.

In order to help others win, you have to assess them and figure out exactly how you can help them. In life, we need to attract that yin-yang with people so that we create a dualism to help each other win. People breathe in oxygen and breathe out carbon dioxide.

Trees breathe in carbon dioxide. Notice how both relationships work together harmoniously.

I remember a time in my military career as a senior Army leader when I was not a confident leader. I had two Army Command Sergeants Major mentors. Command Sergeant Major (CSM) Far and Command Sergeant Major (CSM) Close. As a frocked Sergeant Major, I was uncertain of what I needed to do to be a confident leader. CSM Far taught how to become an assured Sergeant Major. He taught me how to be the bull or the Pretty Boy Mayweather. In one example, CSM Far and I were walking around Fort Bragg and we run across these two officers with enlisted reenlistment gear. Once CSM Far saw this he went ballistic. He cusses, asking the officers where they get the gear from. The officers explained that it came from the reenlistment Noncommissioned Officer (NCO). Once CSM Far heard this he exploded and explained to the officers that the reenlistment NCO should not have done that, and he was going to have a strong conversation with the NCO about what he did wrong. The officers were very remorseful and insisted that they would give the gear back, but CSM Far told them they were fine and to carry on with what they were doing. He would deal with that NCO.

Once the officer's left, I asked CSM Far why he exploded the way that he did. He explained that he was not going to talk to the reenlistment NCO at all, but he wanted to let the officers know that the gear was intended for enlisted soldiers, and them having it was a favor done by that NCO. He essentially put another deposit into the NCO's account.

I learned from that situation, sometimes you have to put on a show to get your point across.

CSM Close taught me how to be smooth, Money Mayweather. I remember a situation where we were all at a change of command ceremony, and it was freezing outside. For practices, we could be in coat and gloves, but for the actual rehearsal, we could not. CSM Close noticed that a Brigade Commander was still in his coat and gloves. CSM Close walked up to the Brigade Commander and nicely asked him to take his coat and gloves off. The Brigade Commander responded no. CSM Close again suggested that he remove the coat and gloves. The officer said because he was a Brigade Commander with a rank that was superior to that of the CSM – he would not remove the gear. CSM Close said he understood the difference between the rank and the officer could take his gear off because the CSM asked, or he could wait until the General arrived and be directed to take it off. The officer took off the jacket. CSM Close taught me how to be a leader who got things done by asking and suggesting. We need not confuse our position and someone's rank. Think of food servers and cooks, versus the manager of the restaurant. Who has more influence on the food served at our tables?

There are three easy steps to aid you in winning. Winning is a fluid situation, it changes based on your perception of what reaching your goal looks like. One: Confidence is a key ingredient. We can increase our confidence by doing what we say we are going to do. This will build confidence and self-esteem. Two: Celebrate the small wins. This will also ensure that you reach your goals. This positive feedback generates energy and touches the feel-good parts of our brain. Three: surround yourself with those people that lift you up – your cheerleaders. However, also ensure that you have those people in your corner who hold you accountable for your mistakes or lack of action. Those three factors will help you win.

Pretty Vs Money Workbook

1. What three things are you going to do today to build confidence?

_____

_____

_____

_____

_____

_____

_____

a. Do three things to help you get better at that.

_____

_____

_____

_____

_____

_____

2. Find a way to understand why you are not confidence.

_____

_____

_____

_____

_____

_____

_____

a. Make time to understand why and figure out how to change it.

_____

_____

_____

_____

_____

_____

_____

3. What have you quit because of a lack of confidence?

_____

_____

_____

_____

_____

_____

_____

3.

D. A. D. (Decide, Act, Dedicate)

One of the biggest problems that people have in life is not knowing what they want. In order to become the best version of yourself, it is important to figure out what you want. Once you have identified what you want, then you can start to implement D.A.D. (Decide, Act, and Be Dedicated to those actions). Once you implement D.A. D results will occur, it will take time to see the results, but they will happen.

If you want a million dollars all you have to do is get one million people to give you a dollar, it's as simple or as complicated as one makes it. In reality, most of the time getting what we want is easy, people just don't want to put in the work to get there. It takes precision and dedication to make what you want come to fruition. It takes time for the seeds of work/action of what we want to germinate. We have to water and nurture those seeds to get what we want. D.A.D. is crucial to everybody in order to produce results.

While growing up, deciding what I wanted was a bit of a struggle for me. When faced with adversity my initial response was to run from it. I can vividly recall one of the times I ran away from my problems. This was around 1982 and I was about 18 or 19 years old at the time. I had been in college for about two years and was "madly in love". Unfortunately, she did not share the same sentiment. I recall telling her I wanted to be more than friends, and she was not having any of that... I can remember it clearly because that was around the time that Prince was extremely popular. One of my favorite song of his "Why You Want To Treat Me So Bad" was out, and it summed up how I was feeling. I can remember playing a lot of Prince during that loss. Prince's music was on constant rotation. I would lay on the bed in the fetal position and listen to his love songs of pain and disappointment.

After that heartbreak, I felt dejected and rejected. Honestly, I didn't feel loved. The sad truth was, when she told me she didn't want me, I could hear what society was telling me again, and again – I wasn't good enough.

I saw myself as an unattractive, unwanted, dark-skinned African-American male.

Remember, I grew up in a time where the Klu Klux Clan held meetings every week, and proudly advertised their meetings. The KKK routinely marched on Sundays in their full garb handing out their newspaper and paraphernalia. I grew up in the late 60s early 70s in the Deep South.

South Carolina was my first major educational experience, and it deeply affected my foundation for formal and informal learning. I was taught the darker the person the less value they held. I heard sentiment for many years. I was taught that I wasn't enough throughout my childhood by society; society demonstrated it over and over. My mother on the other hand, told me I was a King and could have anything that I desired. Hearing is one thing and experiencing is another. For instance, someone saying they love you and showing you that they do makes a difference. If someone gifts you a dozen roses every two days as a way to show they care, we understand that they do.

The scars that I was emotionally entangled with as a child, cut deep. The scars of feeling unworthy negatively affected me. Those wounds made it easier for me to quit when things got hard because in my mind, I wasn't good enough so why try?

As I lay in my bunk bed crying my heart out, the pressures of my situation started to overwhelm me. I'm unloved, in college away from family, and running out of money. I was working a 25 hour a week minimum-wage job and not doing well with my grades I became distracted and dishearten with many things in my life.

At that point, I made the decision to join the Army—quitting yet again. I rationalizing that joining the Army would solve all my problems. It would help me pay for my life and my way ahead. My plan, in my head, was after two years of being in the Army, I would go to Officer Candidate School and become an officer then retire and never be poor or "work" again. So, I enlisted in the Army, I had two years of college under my belt and I was awarded the rank of Private First class.

Once I made the decision to join the military, I

didn't truly realize the new journey and trajectory my life would take. I needed to make a change, I acted on that decision and enlisted, the next step was to be dedicated to the decisions I made. I had done a D.A.D.

My underlying struggles, however, made it difficult for me to be successful in my new venture. I was still who I was (Mindset); who society told me I was. But, the struggle between what society said and what my mom planted in me as a child was starting to manifest. Eventually, my mom's words won, but that is a story for the next book.

In my life up to that point, I had a history of quitting. I quit the football team and the track team, Aikido, hard courses, and at times, I quit on my dreams. If I didn't receive that immediate gratification from whatever venture I was doing, I quit.

I, however, did get that instant gratification from fighting—I was pretty good at that. I got this reputation of being a "bad ass" near the end of middle school. I would fight at the drop of a hat, and I would fight anyone and I do mean "anyone". This aggression stemmed from my feelings of inadequacies and rejection.

I wanted to be loved, but I didn't know how to love myself, and because of that, my go-to was to run. The South taught me that I was less than, and I believed it, which was worse than being taught it—I bought it.

In the 60s and 70s, my skin color didn't afford me a life of equality, fairness, or privilege of any kind. And because I didn't deal with my feelings about myself well, I constantly ran into roadblocks that led me back to the feeling that "I wasn't good enough". Mind Shift matters most in changing our lives and our outcomes. Mindset is also our identity—it is who WE say we are.

When I joined the Army the need to quit when things got hard followed me at first. However, because the Army instilled discipline, responsibility, and being a member of a team, I learned how to counteract the desire to quit. It was hard for me to give up my "quitting" attitude; once my mindset changed, I changed.

I discovered through my trials and tribulations that I had worth, power, and abilities. I was told what I wanted, what I would do, and for how long I would do it, for many weeks during basic training. I was then placed in charge of the team heading to Advance Individual Training at Fort Sam Houston, TX, and I excelled.

After two years in the military, I had the opportunity to become an officer. I took the test passed it with flying colors, and I started building my packet for school. However, in the process of making that life-changing decision, I quit again. My Mindset told me I was not officer material. Can you see the pattern re-emerging? I once again continued the self-destructive pattern of quitting when things got hard. I had not fully replaced the "habit" of quitting yet.

Subconsciously, I didn't think I was worthy of becoming an officer. Sometimes, we don't peruse the things we say we want because we don't think we deserve them. Changing our Mindset from a scarcity mindset to an abundance Mindset is critical to our progress in life. I call this a Mindset shift or a Mind Shift. My identity (Mindset) said that I wasn't worthy, and my actions manifested that thought process – quitting. Also, understanding the caste and class systems of the military (environment) also reinforced this identity (Mindset).

For example, I didn't look at the other side of the pay scale until I was a Sergeant First Class. In the military, we have a published pay chart that has the three different categories of service members of the military listed on one chart.

I was taught to stay in my lane in the military and that is what I did. I was told not to go "to the dark side" (becoming and officer) so I didn't. I didn't peruse an opportunity that I know I would have excelled at because society told me to stay where I was – and I obeyed. Did I know what I wanted? I don't think I did.

After I decided I wasn't going to be an officer, I was aimless. At the rank of Specialist, I just decided to continue to purposelessly be in the Army. I had no direction or motivation to do more than what I was doing, and honestly, I wasn't so great at my job, anyway. I was mediocre until I got fired.

After I was fired, I was put in the right place and my career excelled. I got confirmation from others that I was worthy and that was the jump start I needed for my Mind Shift.

I was a dental laboratory technician. I made crowns, dentures, and bridges. I worked very hard at that job, seven days a week for many years. I would work a half a day on Saturday and two hours on Sunday to ensure that I got the job done. The truth of the matter, however, was that I was not very good at my job. A crown that should have taken twenty minutes to insert took the dentist well over an hour to place it.

After a while of putting up with my mediocre quality of work, the dentist pulled me aside and told me that he was going to move me. Which basically meant that I was fired. I was not successfully accomplishing the mission. Sure enough, a couple of weeks later I was moved out of that position and became the Administrative Specialist for the Operations and Training section. From there, I just exploded into excellence.

People started talking to me about how to wear the uniform, how to pass boards, and how to conduct ceremonies. I became the regulation guru, and that became my first venture into leadership, which then transferred to the mentoring of people.

My getting fired from a job that I was mediocre at, set me on a course of excellence for the rest of my career. Being fired from that job gave me the opportunity to shine.

After I became a Sergeant First Class, many leaders started grooming me for Sergeant Major. I didn't think much about that as I was still in my lane, however; their encouragement eventually made me see that it was possible for me.

Earlier in my career, I needed external motivation and confirmation and that I was good at my craft. As I've developed and revised my own philosophies, I realized that I am the source (Mindset) of that stimuli.

We all need some outside stimuli to reassure and reignite our thought processes and confirm that we are heading in the right direction. As time has gone on, I have needed that ignition less and less. The getting fired was the catalyst for me being put in the right place. I found my seat, and that helped me explode into new levels of excellence.

After I got fired, I made Sergeant, and Staff Sergeant, in reasonable time. I was finally in the right seat and the Mind Shift started taking place. I made Sergeant First Class and Master Sergeant, and Sergeant Major in the secondary zone. It took two looks to make the Command Sergeant Major (CSM) list. I then became a Nominative CSM my second-time at-bat. I ended my military career on my terms, as a Two Star Level CSM. I held one of the most prestigious positions of my career field because I started using the D.A.D. principles.

Often we don't make decisions because we don't know what we want. And when you ask for things; they aren't really what you want. Not taking the time to truly asses what you want can be detrimental to our success.

I did a coaching session recently, and the person expressed a desire to make a move to start a new life elsewhere. I told him that he had to decide where he wanted to be and what he wanted to do before he got there. He expressed that they wanted to move to Texas but had no idea what he wanted to do when he got there for employment. Then, I asked what pay point he wanted, and I asked what kind of work would bring in that type of money. He had not thought of these questions.

The first step in changing your circumstance is to truly know what you want and to map out the way to your future destination. Starting with the end in mind. Decide!!!!

After the decision is made the next step is to Act upon that decision. Do those things that will support your decision or stop doing those things that hurt that decision. Making a decision is great but now the hard part comes in – how to get to where you want to be.

I told my client to put in two applications a day for the next thirty days, in Texas and at the pay grade and level that he wanted. The action creates momentum, synergy, and vibrations which pulls the actions, ideas, and people that you need towards you. Act!!!!

I told him to continue putting in two applications a day for the next thirty days. I know you will get tired, but keep on putting in the applications. Dedication is required to get the action accomplished and get the results from those actions. Be Dedicated!!!!

When I retired from the Army, I was in the lower half of the economic food chain for the military. I was part of the other cast/class that was not the top. I was at the top of the lower half, but still in the lower half.

I decided that the next level that I worked at – I would be in the senior half of that sector. I told myself I would not accept anything less than that. I told myself, which level of employment I was going to get, and I ensured I did everything in my power to get the job I desired.

I applied for jobs only at the level I wanted. I knew in my heart what my worth was and I went from it. I let nothing and no one deter me from what I knew I was capable of. And trust me, there were those that told me I was not worthy.

I decided what I wanted, acted upon that decision and was dedicated to that pursuit. Once I was hired, I negotiated the price point I wanted.

I have a number in my head for how much money I want to make at the end of every year. As the years have progressed, that number has increased. The decision about the dollar number I want influences many of the actions that I take. But, my biggest pull is the relationships that I build or the personal connections I make in my vocation. These relationships really get me going and they ensure I get the desired effects in my life.

I implemented the D.A.D. philosophy to get that job. I had the price point that I wanted along with the job level that I desired. I put in 60 applications for a month and only applied for jobs that fit the criteria that I knew I deserved. I got seventeen referrals, five job interviews, and three firm offers. The law of number's works. It doesn't matter what you want when the effort is put in place what you desire will come into existence at some point in time.

Here is another example that eventually worked the way it was supposed to work.

I was the keynote speaking engagement in December 2018. I told the audience by this time next year I wanted my wife to have a brand-new Mercedes

SUV. This year, 2019, I didn't meet that goal. However, here is what I did meet, I paid off the current Mercedes more than a year early. And you know what, she really didn't want another car. I wanted it for her, but she didn't really want it. I hope you got that—It was my desire, not her desire.

Even though I didn't get the car I wanted my wife to have, I moved so much farther ahead in other areas. Sometimes what we want isn't what God knows is best for us. Instead of having another car; I have extra dollars in my bank account to do something even more positive. The journey is more important than the destination.

When we quit at the first sign of adversity, maybe, we are not worthy of the things we say we want. Or, maybe it isn't what we really want. Time is the most valuable thing that we "possess". We have all the time in the world, but we have only the time of this world. And this lifetime is limited.

We must be assertive, even aggressive, at times, on the things in life we want, but at the same time be patient in waiting for those things to come to fruition. We have to be hungry but at the same time satisfied with where we are. That is a tough place to be in, but the end results are limitless.

There is plenty for everyone because everyone does not want the same thing. However, to become the best version of yourself you must first Decide, Act, and Be dedicated to those actions and you will get the results you seek. You will grow and those around you will grow. Apply the D.A.D principle to your life.

D.A.D. (Decide, Act, Dedicate) Workbook

1. What do You want?

_____

_____

_____

_____

_____

_____

_____

b. Then what do you want inside of the three key areas of Relationships, Health and Wealth?

_____

_____

_____

_____

_____

_____

_____

c. If you can't figure out what you want: Think about your pay points, the areas that you are dissatisfied with, what do "Ideals" look like to you.

_____

_____
_____
_____
_____

_____

2. What are you going to do to get to what to what you want?

_____
_____
_____
_____
_____
_____

_____

b. What Price are you willing to pay?

_____
_____
_____
_____
_____
_____

_____

3. Who or what holds you accountable to reach your goals?

_____
_____
_____
_____

_____

_____

_____

b. What revisions are necessary, if any ?

_____

_____

_____

_____

_____

_____

_____

4.

Your Gifts Are Not Yours

Our gifts are those things we are good at effortlessly. My gift is my voice. I know that when I stand at the podium, the words I speak WILL motivate and uplift others. I pride myself on my ability to command a room and my gift of motivating others.

It's easy to believe things won't change. We become complacent, sometimes even overconfident in our abilities and gifts. We often get trapped into thinking we will "forever" be in command of our Gift. Even if we don't verbalize these subconscious thoughts, we still have them. It's like how almost everyone thinks they have "tomorrow." For some, "tomorrow" will not come. I was of that Mindset – the one that I would have my gift forever until I was tested.

One definition of the word test is "an event or situation that reveals the strength or quality of someone or something by putting them under strain." In school, we usually prepare for tests. We study hard and practice to ensure that we get the best possible grade. That is in school.

But what happens when you don't know that you are being tested? How do you excel when you don't realize that you are in the middle of a test? A TRUE test in life is one that you don't know you are going through, and you didn't see coming. That kind of test defines the way the rest of your life is lived.

What happens when things challenge the way we see ourselves; when adversity strikes? In September 2018, the very thing that I knew I was good at became a burden. I went from motivating others to shying away from speaking engagements and people in general. I still had my gift of speaking, but my personal life somehow got in the way of me being able to do the very thing that made me who I was. My gift became a burden.

Once I exited the military, I set goals to help me transition. The three most important goals I wanted to nourish were my relationships, my health, and my wealth. Now that I had more time, fitness was the easiest of the three. Relationships and wealth, while not extremely difficult required a little more work that the fitness goal.

I wanted to propel myself financially, so I implemented different tactics to get me where I wanted to be. One of the things that I did was change my surroundings. I started associating myself with people in the tax bracket that I wanted to be in. My mind-set was, and still is, "in order to think greater, I had to associate myself with those that DID bigger and thought even more advanced than I DID."

In September 2018, I was at a financial conference in Atlanta with six of my new associates. This trip, I think, was the start of the events that changed the way the rest of my life was lived. While on this trip and traveling from place to place I noticed – one of my colleagues in the car, I rode in had a bad and noticeable upper and lower respiratory infection.

About two months later, still, on my journey of self-improvement, my health changed. I felt a need to take a deeper breath. Not that I had a shortness of breath, I just generally felt the need to take a deeper breath about every 1 ½ minutes.

I still ran the five miles as usual; however, I felt the needed to inhale a little more than I thought was normal. I gave it a few weeks and thought maybe the symptoms would lessen, but they stayed the same.

Finally, in December 2018, I went to a doctor to see what the issue was. I thought that maybe I had pneumonia or asthma, as I had asthma as a child. The doctor, in turn, ordered a chest x-ray and found nothing. However, my issue was still there – this needs to take a deeper breath about every 1 ½ minutes.

About a month later, I was still having the same issue, so my primary care doctor ordered a CT scan. The doctor informed me that he would contact me on Friday. Well, Friday came and went with no call, so I went into my own records to see what the CT scan concluded. My life, from that moment forward, was forever changed. The "Test" had begun.

The results from the radiologist stated that I had a large mass on my right lung, and that lung cancer couldn't be ruled out; however, there was a slight possibility that it could be an infection. I tried to remain calm even though I had not received a phone call from my doctor. On Monday, I received the call from the doctor's office stating that they needed to see me as soon as possible. Having read the results, I already knew what information was in the record, but I wanted to remain optimistic.

The doctor stated that he wanted me to do another CT scan with contrast so that they could have a clearer picture of what was actually going on in my lungs. Their thought process for the dye with sugar was, that the spot would light up if it was a cancerous mass on the CT scan.

It took almost a month to get the CT scan appointment, and in that time frame, I became even more withdrawn. I didn't tell my friends or my family what was going on with me. I did not tell my wife, my son, my mother, my brother, or my dad. I started to internalize my feelings and emotions even more. The only person that I talked to at length was the unit chaplain because we were and still are good friends.

When we are put under pressure, who we are, becomes even more apparent. Pressure, like wealth, displays who a person really is. By most of my nature am an introverted, solitary person. I became that even more with those who did not see me on a routine basis.

My thoughts started drifting to my mortality. The life expectancy for stage 4 lung cancer was about 4 months according to Dr. Google." My primary-care doctor told me to be positive, and that he didn't think it was cancer. I continued to exercise and pushed myself to achieve my goals. The entire time, I still felt the need to take those deeper breaths. I knew that something was going on and that knowledge affected me the most.

I had to take a trip to Oklahoma and while there; I received a call from the oncology pulmonary clinic. I spoke with a lung cancer specialist. The lung cancer specialist contacted me about the procedure I need to undergo for them to check my lungs and see how extensive the damage really was.

I started doing research, and I learned that, according to the CDC, "more people in the United States die from lung cancer than any other type of cancer. This is true for both men and women." Furthermore, black males are the demographics with the highest rate of lung cancer.

While I am experiencing all this internal turmoil, a new soldier arrived at the unit. She was also suffering with lung cancer at the age of 31. We talked about the issue, and I told her about my anxiety, and how I am feeling because of the diagnoses.

By this time, I already started shutting down. I stop reaching out to people. I no longer did my monthly newsletter, and I completely shut out friends and because more attentive to my internal family and friends. I saved a voicemail from a friend of mine who's church I was to speak at. I still vividly remember his concern when he spoke, he asked where I had been, and if I had fallen off the face of the earth. I later had a powerful conversation and gave a heartfelt presentation at his church.

A month later, I finally got scheduled for my CT with contrast. I was escorted into a little room with little chairs and I honestly felt suffocated. There was another woman with me that was experiencing the same procedure, her name was Mrs. Johnson. I had decided what was going to be for me, was to be for me, and if it was my time than I would deal with that. I was still concerned with if I had done enough. I wondered if it was my time, would my family be taken care of. I was also concerned with them knowing that I loved them. I also wondered would my legacy be secure. I did not fear death and still don't—I fear that I have not done enough.

Once both of us got done with our CT Scan, we were again placed in a little room to wait on our results. When the technician finally arrived, he spoke to Mrs. Johnson jovially and stated her doctor would get back to her shortly. His tone with me, however, was not the same as it had been with her. His tone towards me was very somber.

I again went into my records to look at my test results. I would love to say that everything was clear and there were no bright spots, but I can't. Two bright spots were lit up on my right lung. So my thought process shifted, and I started thinking about how I was going to tell the ones that I loved that for seven months I had been keeping this enormous secret from them. I also started thinking about making plans and life term care. All the things we should all prepare for, but who really thinks at fifty-five their life may be at its end.

Mostly, I felt overwhelmed at how behind the power curve I was. I finally decide to break down and tell my wife. I now have no choice because I have a biopsy scheduled, and I need her by my side. In telling her,

I made the decision that I had to stop trying to bear all this alone and allow my friends and family to be there for me. The biopsy was in March 2019, three days before my birthday.

The day of the biopsy everything was taking three times as long as they initially said it would. I sat in the preparation room for about four hours with my wife just thinking about all the possibilities that could occur. There was a procedure going on in the operatory next to me and I could hear almost everything.

The woman in the room next to me was having a lung biopsy and after the procedure, I heard the doctors ask her was she okay; she responded yes, and that was the last I heard from her for a while. She then complained about discomfort in breathing. The surgical staff was brought back in to assess and treat. She had a pneumothorax, this is where air leaks out between the lung and chest cavity. It can make it hard to breathe or can cause your lung to collapse. Her husband was contacted, and she was admitted to the ICU for further observation. This was not comforting for the patient in the next room to hear, that patient was—me.

I was told that there could be complications, that a blood clot, pneumonia or a pneumothorax might be one of them. Understanding that is one thing, but to hear it happening beside me was another situation entirely—I was up next, just praying to God that the odds were in my favor.

Up until that point, residents had treated me and prepped me. After the procedure, the credentialed specialist woke me up and explains to me that based on his 30 years of experience, he saw no cancer in my lungs. However, he could not be certain until the lab results came back. I also checked my records, and it came back that there were no issues with my lungs. Conversely, the aftermath of the decisions I made during my turmoil still had a lasting effect. Later reflecting on that moment, it hit me; I let a lot of people down! I was selfish; I stopped utilizing my Gift in a time when people needed it. I negated my Gift because it got harder to use. I was selfish by not using my Gift to help others; in reality, I was hurting people.

That is when I came to the realization that our Gifts are not ours. Our gifts are not for us, they are to uplift and help others in their time of need, hurt, pain, joy, happiness or excitement.

Motivating and inspiring others can be very cathartic for them as well as for me. Our gifts are like seeds. Alone a seed does nothing, but when you plant, water, and provide it with light—the magic happens, and it flourishes. Once planted and nurtured, a seed provides value. If it's not watered and pruned as well as utilizes it atrophies. Here is my question for you: Are you using your gifts, and if you aren't why?

Your Gifts Workbook

1. What's your Gift?

_____
_____
_____
_____
_____
_____

_____

a. Ease vs Challenges?

_____
_____
_____
_____
_____
_____

_____

2. How are you using it?

_____
_____
_____
_____
_____
_____

_____

b. If you aren't, why??

_____

_____

_____

_____

_____

_____

_____

c. Is your lack of usage hurting others?

_____

_____

_____

_____

_____

_____

_____

3. What are you going to do to improve on your gift?

_____

_____

_____

_____

_____

_____

_____

5.

It's Not Okay to Stay Where You Are

Imagine what you want, because believe it or not, you can have everything you want. We doubt ourselves. We say that we want this life, this house, this car, but we make no strides to get to where we want to be. Maybe we don't take action because we don't believe we can get there – because we haven't seen it yet. The first step to seeing is to grasp it and lock it inside of our minds. Thoughts and ideas are visions. We just have to find a way to manifest them into reality.

Things in this world are created twice, once in the mind and once in the physical. As we are spiritual beings, we create things in our heads, minds, and vibrations. Afterwards, we can visualize them and create them in the physical. Only then we can touch and feel them. Seeing what we want in our mind is the first steps to achieving our goals. Know that everything in life comes with a price. Nothing is given away. We have to decide how far we are ready to go to fulfil our goal, dream, or purpose. Are YOU willing to go the distance? You are limited only by your thought process. Times have changed, and so must we. Change is the only constant.

Growing up, I was the "remote control". When I

was younger, I was told to get up and change the dial channel. TVs had dials back then. Now, when I ask my nephews do, they know what a remote control is, they say, "yeah, but we don't use it."

It's astonishing to me how things have changed over the years. I remember the start of many things because I grew up in the 60s, and it was a turbulent time in the United States. So when I say anything, and everything is attainable I say it because I know.

I remember when color TV became mainstream, it's astonishing to me that, now we have virtual reality. Most things that are commonplace today, were mere thoughts in those days. However, there will always be one person that can see the bigger, different picture than current reality. Someone who understands, even if it's impossible now, tomorrow it will be probable.

Be that person for yourself. Reinvent your own will, and learn to live in your purpose, regardless of the current reality. Just because it's impossible now, doesn't mean it is improbable. We can and must change our mindset.

Nothing is impossible. We have the ability to manifest our destiny. Sometimes we are more interested in instant gratification than doing the work to reach our destination. We can have it all, just not right now. That may sound like a contradiction, but it goes back to my original saying, nothing in life is free.

What we think is impossible today is only a thought process, because someone hasn't done it yet! Think about that. What do you want to do to break the glass ceiling? Do you realize that 2020 will be the next decade? Look back on all the things we have witnessed in your generation. Things are constantly evolving, are you? Are you truly living in your purpose? Where do you want to see yourself ten years from now? If it's not of you fulfilling your destiny, why? You have to take steps to get there.

I was a Sergeant First Class (SFC) and the Noncommissioned Officer in Charge of a dental clinic when I began to visualize my destiny. Everyone kept telling me that it was my destiny to be a Command Sergeant Major (CSM), but I couldn't see it. Eventually, it finally sunk in, maybe if others see greatness in me, I can be great. The emotional aspect of my wanting to be a CSM stemmed from my treatment as a Private First Class. I remember my time in Korea having to sit in the back of a vehicle with the equipment while it was freezing outside, all because I was a "lower" enlisted soldier. There was room for me to have a seat in the cab of the vehicle, but because of my rank, I wasn't allowed to sit inside the heat. I vowed to myself when I could be in charge, I would make sure no one was treated the way that I was.

That emotional memory propelled me to achieve the highest paygrade possible for an enlisted soldier in the United States Army. Once I was given the encouragement that I would be a great CSM as an SFC I could visualize me achieving that goal. I could see the result that I wanted. I wanted to change the face and structure of the Army. I could visualize me purposefully affecting change in the Army. Once you know your dream, find a picture that represents what you want, so that you have a constant reminder of your dream. That picture will hold you accountable when times get hard.

Once I decided I wanted to be a CSM I had two additional ranks that I needed to acquire to reach my goal. Your purpose is just the first step to your ultimate objective. Once you realize what you want, you must put plans in motion to get there. I talked to people that were already ahead of me. I surrounded myself with those in higher positions than I and asked them how they got to where they were. They would always tell me that I needed to take care of soldiers. So I started developing a plan to emulate what they expressed. I observed what helped them be successful, but I also used my knowledge and intellect to mould their style into my own. Change does not happen overnight. However, once you implement a plan for your future, you will be more inclined to stay focused and see it through. When you focus on your goals, they become visible and attainable.

How do you see yourself at your finish line? Can you truly see what you want? The price that you must pay to get to where you want, is individualized. The word "PRICE" is also subjective. That price can be as simple as money, or as grand as time. Whatever your worth is to you, is what you are willing to give of yourself. There is a price you must pay to get to where you want to be.

When I decided to be a CSM, the price that I paid was my time. I invested my time into people so that they knew that I was there for them. I guaranteed that they were effectively taken care of. I invested in people, and the result was the organization we worked for changing for the better. People saw and understood that, and eventually, when I gained the position of CSM, I knew that I was worthy of that position. I took the time to do the things to get there.

Imagine what you want and remember there are no limits or right or wrong answers. God made us filled with a purpose. What does that purpose look like for you? What cost are you willing to concede? Nothing is free, time, energy, money, and connections all cost.

Nevertheless, if you don't know what you want, and you don't know the lengths that you are will go to reach your goal, you will never get there. That lack of knowledge will impede your progress toward understanding and knowing your purpose.

It is not okay to stay where you are! Nothing is impossible, if you are at the same place, you are today in the year 2030, you probably have failed yourself. This applies to your physical, economic, and emotional being.

The things we think are impossible today, will be a grain of sand in the future because everything changes. Your restricted reality is based on your limited thinking. Often times, we don't have what we want because we either think that we are unworthy, or we believe that it's impossible to reach our goals. Positive thinking and affirmations are among the first steps to adjust that Mindset.

Where You Are Workbook

1. Imagine what you want.

_____

_____

_____

_____

_____

_____

_____

2. What will you do to get to where you want to be?

_____

_____

_____

_____

_____

_____

b. What price will you pay?

_____

_____

_____

_____

_____

_____

3. Can you see the end / see yourself getting there?

_____

_____
_____
_____
_____
_____
_____
_____

6.

Why, Want, Waste

In order to achieve excellence, you must first understand what your "why" is. I often talk about "the why." Let's delve deeper into it. If your why is strong enough you will figure out your HOW. Your "why" will push you towards whatever your goal you are trying to meet. You will be propelled to whatever vision you are called to make a reality.

One of my "whys" motivated me to attain Sergeant First Class in the US Army in the secondary zone. I wanted that promotion, but not for me, it was for my newborn son. My boy was my "why". His existence motivated me to shift my mindset. I became disciplined, which helped me move to the next level in my career.

Before his birth, I wasn't progressing as rapidly as I should have. His birth provided me with a "why" which allowed me to get to the next level in my career, and I did it quickly.

I saw a bigger picture and a greater vision; I wanted him to have someone he could and would be proud to call Dad.

With the promotion to Sergeant First Class came a boost in rank and pay. I knew that it would also help me provide better for my son and family. Growing up, I did not experience that.

My "why" was Ben, my son. I knew I would do what needed to be done and stay on that cause until I became successful. I studied harder, learned more, applied actions and achieved more – all because I knew where I wanted to be. I knew where I had to be! I focused on immediate achievements; This was the foundation for me attaining my "why". What is your "why"?

Wanting to provide more for my family stemmed from my childhood. I grew up without, and I didn't want my son to have to do the same. I wanted him to have as many options as possible. I did want him to want, and to struggle a bit, because there is something magical in that. The hard things we go through will help us grow through, but I also wanted there to be that security around him. I wanted him to have economic freedom. I wanted him to be situated in a powerful manner. I knew my promotion to Sergeant First Class was a gateway to seeing my vision become a reality. I had a vision, but I was also shortsighted at the same time. That, however, is a story for the next book.

When I was thirteen years old, we lived in a small one-bathroom, two-bedroom apartment. I distinctly remember the sliding glass doors that served as our back door. Not too far from our back door, there was a gas station.

I don't recall what it was, but there was something that we didn't have. I don't know if it was milk, bread, eggs, or one of those staples – I just can't recall what it was. However, I remember how depleted I felt because of not having it. I remember the sadness and shame I felt in my soul. I can recall standing in our small apartment crying for the thing that I longed for. Not weeping, but crying because we didn't have enough money to do what we needed to do. I distinctly remember saying, I will never be this poor again.

From that point forward, at the age of 13, I started working. I did whatever I needed to do to make money. I pumped gas (at that very same gas station I looked at every day), cut grass, and even took nails out of the dock, I also served as a busboy at Shoney's. From the moment I told myself, I would at no time be that poor again, I never was. And a great part of my "why" stemmed from not wanting my son to ever be in that situation. My "why" drove me to become successful, it also pushed me to figure out how.

There is something so magical about having the desire to "want" something. There is something transcendent about "wanting" to get to that next level. That want is crucial in helping us get to the subsequent future that we long for – to make our vision into a reality.

"Want" sometimes gets a bad rap. We are told that we shouldn't want much more than what we have, or what we are. We are often taught to that "want" can be evil, that it is being greedy, dirty, or even wrong to desire things. I am not here to debate that, but I submit to you, no matter your point of view, it can be a catalyst to success.

A "want" for me was being able to set the example

of success for my son. I have succeeded and failed miserably at this. You must have a "want" in order to push yourself. That "want" combined with your why, will allow you to unlock the extraordinary, even the truly exceptional. The "want" for me was having my son be able to do and have more than I could imagine. I also wanted to set that example of achievement for him. When we see others getting to where we want to go, or to where we want to be, we realize that it is possible to get there. Therefore, the success of others can be my success, or maybe it is also my success.

On the opposite end of Why and Want is Waste. We waste time, money, and energy (health) more than anything else. These wasted elements lead to a loss of potential and realization of a better future.

We waste time. And like I continue to say, we have all the time in the world, but we only have the time in THIS world. We can only do what we can accomplish in this life. If we waste the time we have, we have wasted our lives.

We waste money and we only have a certain amount of that.

We waste our energy as well, and as we progress in the age that also depletes. I will submit to you that you waste a lot more than you think you do. Think about what you want and don't have. What are you wasting that could help you to achieve your goals? In a month's time, I waste about 40 hours playing a video game. I get great enjoyment out of it, but I am also addicted to it. Once I start, it is so hard to stop. I know that time could be better served elsewhere. I need relaxation time (fun time) and I have to take that sometimes so that I can accomplish my goals. I set limits on how much I can play to meet my need for relaxation, and the rest of that time is a waste. If we eliminate the waste in our lives, we could have more of the things we want.

Why, Want, Waste used in the proper manner can and will help us to achieve our goals. If you don't know your why, figure out what drives you. Find what gives you that push to change your status quo. Finding what you want is as simple as acknowledging your burning desire, those things that you obsess over in a positive manner. The "how" helps you to figure out who you need to become, to active that goal. This will, in turn, lead to you getting the things you desire. Your why is that pull in your gut that drives you to be better than before; that want drives you to get there. The why also provides the momentum to help you achieve your goals.

The waste is the opposite end of those two things. We have so much in America that we waste. Think about what you waste, not even material, the energy you waste also takes its toll on you and your health. What can you give up that can help you achieve your goals? The combination of increasing your "Why" and "Want" and decreasing what you "Waste", will help you achieve not only excellence but accelerated excellence.

Why, Want, Waste Workbook

1. What do you want?

_____

_____

_____

_____

_____

_____

2. What emotions and time are you wasting?

_____

_____

_____

_____

_____

a. If you know that you are wasting, what will you do to change this?

_____

_____

_____

_____

_____

_____

_____

3. Who is your accountability partner to make sure you are doing what you say you want to do?

_____

_____

_____

_____

_____

_____

_____

7.

I Am

Let's talk about I Am. Let me ask you a question, is it possible to give someone something you don't have? The answer is no! If you don't have love, you can't give it. The same with money, if you don't have it, you can't give it away. Think about self-esteem. If you don't have a motivational force pushing you forward, you won't ever progress. Inspiration lasts a bit longer than motivation, but both factors derive from the force that propels you forward.

I've continuously said throughout this book, there are three main factors that drive me, they are the most important things in life in the following order; Relationships, Health, and Wealth. Which is why I wholeheartedly say, you can't give what you don't have. If you don't have those three factors, I mentioned above you can't give them away.

Relationships come first. My relationship with God is my main priority, and your relationship with YOUR God should be yours. The next relationship I work on is the one I have is with myself. We talk to ourselves more than we talk to anyone else. In the shower, driving the car, even when cooking our meals, we always have Self-talk going on. Self-talk can make or break us. Self – talk reinforces the mindset and nurtures our identity. So ensure that you are breathing life into yourself. Speak realistically and positively to yourself. If you don't love yourself, how can you truly love anyone else?

Health is my next priority. My health is paramount and comes first. You can't take care of anyone if your health is not where it needs it to be. Next comes the health of your loved ones, and your family members. Health problems can cause issues in relationships. The decisions we make with our health now cannot only affect us but the ones that we love. Make sure you take care of you first, so that you can take care of others. I love what Jim Rohn says about his father, "Son, you come first, right after me." Think about how powerfully true this statement is. Jim also says, "I'll take care of me for you if you'll take care of you for me." When your self-interest comes first, we all win.

Wealth is the last of the three, but that does not mean that it is unimportant. Wealth is the economic engine that runs the world. The bible says to be fruitful. That means that income, and ownership is important. Wealth is not just about taking care of me. It also extends to taking care of my family and my community. I say that to express to you the importance of building your wealth because it is not only for you, but for your family, and your community. You've got to take care of your wealth so that you can help those who you choose to help. Your economic gifts can help so many others, years after you have gone on to the next world. Build your wealth!

This chapter centers on honing and strengthening your relationships, your health, and your wealth. This is done by defining a clear picture of who you are.

I am whoever I say I am, and so are You.

You have heard that saying before; but have you listened to it?

That saying goes back to self-talk.

Who am I?

I am a child of God, and because of that, I get all the fruits, blessings, inheritances and privileges that come with that. I receive all the freedoms that allow me to live in that truth. I walk in that talk. I'm not perfect, but I live in that truth because it is my truth, and you can live in your truth by knowing who you are. You define you.

I am Benjamin H. S. Scott, Jr. I own that name because I bought that name. What is your name? Write your name down right now. Do you realize how much power is in that name? It is magical and beautiful, especially to you. You and your name are unique. There is no one like you, none in the existence of creation. Know that you are special!

I am a husband, father, son, and brother. I am a friend! Who are you, who do you belong to, and who do you want to be? Think about that! Who do you want to be?

Now let's get down to the facts. Why is I Am important? It is a mindset. It consists of your ethics and values. It affects your behavior because it is how you see yourself. If you don't think that you are worth much, guess what your behavior reflects?

Your thoughts become your actions. If you think/tell others this or that always makes me mad, what do your actions reflect? That you are angry.

Let's take the person who is constantly late. They may have the mindset of my time is more significant than others. My needs are more important than yours. My position is so important that other's time is less valuable. This mindset shows up in "always" being late for someone else's "thing."

So, our decisions are based on our mindset as well as our reactions to circumstances. According, to your principles (mindset), is how we behave.

If you don't like your behavior, you won't like your results. If you don't like your results, adjust your behavior. All of these rationalizations are simple, but they are not easy.

How you see yourself is what you will produce. This all goes back to giving. You can't give what you do not have. For example, if you look in a mirror and say you are beautiful, over time you will believe it. Because YOU are. I say that to say, change how you see yourself, and others around you will see you differently as well.

I saw myself as unattractive and unlovable. For many years, I wasn't positive because I didn't believe I was worthy. When I told myself, I could be confident that all changed. I built myself into who I wanted to be.

Positive affirmations along with a strong work ethic will help you to attain your goals. You must be and do in order to have. Affirmations can jumpstart your new way of thinking. If you don't have at least one affirmation about where you want to be, stop what you are doing and make one! Write it down.

You are who you are, understand and embrace that truth. You are self-made. When you are strong in that truth, it will translate and other people will see it. Wake up the "I Am" in you! If you behave the way you want to be, you will eventually become that person. Along the way to becoming that person, "it" will manifest in your reality. You can achieve your heart's desire. Once you figure out your gift, your quality of life, and the quality of life of others around you will improve.

I am the architect of my future. We have all made mistakes, but that is how we have gotten where we are. The Bible says, "And we know that all things work together for good to them that love God, to them who are they called according to his purpose." If we can own our mistakes, we can fix them.

When thinking of the future, look to your tribe, crowd, and friends. If you love what you are doing and who you see there, change nothing. If that is not a true statement for you, change things. It is true that we are the average of the 5 people we spend time with the most.

Some of the people with you now will not be the people that can go where you are going. Look at those you hang with – If they aren't helping you to get to where you want to be, why are they in your life? If they are not adding value, but bring you issues, headache, and drama, why are you texting them?

I Am responsible for where I am. I am Self-Made. My past put me here, and my future is being determined by what I do today.

I Am inspiring. What inspires you? What makes you want to do what you want to do? Whatever it is, you must do whatever it takes to get there.

I Am an overcomer. What do you need to do to overcome? Let what you have to overcome inspire you!

I am disciplined. I have what I have, and I am what I am because of that fact. I know the goals that I want to accomplish, and I will take the time necessary to make them a reality.

You have to take the time to get what you want. Always work on your dream using your gift. No matter how long it takes, put in the effort even if it's just an hour per week.

Your life changes when YOU start to change. Start now!

I am B.E.N. Be Excellent Now. Excellence is defined by you. Define what that means to you. Anytime you feel yourself not being excellent, reinvent yourself and get back in the fight.

I challenge you to be B.E.N. in every situation. Change your behavior to change your results. If you can do and be better, make it happen. If you aren't being the best version of yourself, fix it. There is no time like the present. You have all the time in the world, but only the time of this world. Improve who you are, so that you can help others. And always remember B.E.N.

I Am Workbook

1. What is your Self-Talk saying about you? Look at your results in the 3 Key areas.

_____

_____

_____

_____

_____

_____

_____

2. Are we getting good quality sleep, exercise, eating appropriately and good quality air?

_____

_____

_____

_____

_____

_____

_____

a. How can you utilize your gift to further your progress towards your goal?

_____

_____

_____

_____

_____

_____

_____

3. Who do you need to let go of? What habit will you replace, and what will you replace it with?

_____

_____

_____

_____

_____

_____

_____

Outro

Every chapter in this book had a workbook section. If you didn't do the work or did it "good enough," I challenge you to go back and revisit what you wrote. I ask that you set aside a little time every day to work on You so that you can become who you truly are.

Saying you want to change is one thing, but putting it into action is quite another. I selected those steps because **Being Excellent Now** is something we can all do. Why are you waiting to change your future, when you can start today? B.E.N. is a prelude of things to come. B.E.N. is absolutely achievable – perfection is not.

Each chapter focuses on being excellent. Deciding, Acting, and being Dedicated to those actions focuses on not quitting. I Am, talks about knowing who you are so that you can have the right mindset. If you realize that your mindset needs to change, now is the time to adjust your way of thinking. Your gift, is about taking the gift that God, has given you, and using them to make the world around you better. Each chapter focuses on honing those skills so that you can get to the next level in your life. Once you have reached that level, figure out what comes next for you, and continue to excel. Always remember that the sky is the limit for you!

When you figure out what you want, you can figure

out what you have to think and do to get it. Next, decide what price and time you are willing to pay or invest to arrive at your desired destination.

Once you understand your gift, know that your gift is meant to help others get to where they need to be. Your excellence is not only your own, but it is there to help others get to the next level. We are building and changing the world—our world-first but then the butterfly effect takes over. We change and build each day, each moment, by Being Excellent Now. My hope is that you take what I have written, read it, and apply it. Work what works for you at this time. If it works now, work it, if not, discard it for now, but come back to it later. As long as you have found a morsel of change for the better, and are motivated to take some action, I have done my job.

God bless, and Be, Excellent, Now.

About The Author

Benjamin H. S. Scott, Jr. entered the United States Army in 1983 and served more than 32 years cumulating as a Command Sergeant Major at the 2-star level. He earned the 3rd highest military award given in peacetime by the Army-the Distinguished Service Medal and the Bronze Star for meritorious service in a combat zone. While in the Army, he served his country in Iraq, Afghanistan, Germany, and six states of the United States of America.

Ben is an Executive Director with The John Maxwell Group; a certified Coach, Trainer, and Speaker, a certified Army Medical Department Arbinger Facilitator, a trained Lean Leader, Certified Scrum Master, an Army Medical Department Certified Lean Six Sigma Black Belt Candidate, and a member of The American College of Healthcare Executives. He is the CEO of Ben Scott LLC, a company dedicated to inspiring others through meaningful connections to a tight circle of diverse and influential people. Ben Scott LLC speaks, teaches, coaches, and trains people and organizations to excel through helping individual and groups achieve and succeed.

He obtained his Series 7 license also known as the General Securities Representative Exam from the Financial Industry Regulatory Authority (FINRA); a Bachelor's Degree (Cum Laude) in Business from

Saint Leo University and only has to complete his capstone project for his Master's Degree in Management and Leadership from Webster University. He serves as the President of a non-profit, Raising Up the Lowcountry. He served on the board of directors of the Belvoir Credit Union, Secretary and Treasurer of the Hunter Ridge Homeowners Association and as an intern/fellow with the Senate Armed Services Committee's subcommittee on personnel.

He is a Transition Expert ~ who will help you transition from where you are to the next level, however "YOU" define that next level.

Connect with him at **www.BenScottLLC.com**

Made in the USA
Columbia, SC
14 October 2024

43551585R00048